IMPERFECT
Self-Love

A Collection of Poems, Quotes & Affirmations

Keisha A. Bloise
THE LOVE SCIENTIST

Copyright © 2021 ALL RIGHTS RESERVED.

No part of this book may be reproduced in any written, electronic, recording, or photocopying without written permission of the publisher or author. The exception would be in the case of brief quotations embodied in the critical articles or reviews and pages where permission is specifically granted by the publisher or author.

Cover By: TamikaInk.com

Formatting: Carla M. Dean, U Can Mark My Word Editorial Services

Photographer: Ciara Smith

Library of Congress Cataloging-in-Publication Data has been applied for.

ISBN: 978-1-7370120-6-1

PRINTED IN THE UNITED STATES OF AMERICA.

Dedication

In loving memory of my beautiful mother and angel, Marjorie Kaye Cooke (May 27, 1958 – Sept. 1, 2017).

I'll forever be grateful for being blessed
with your sweet, fiery spirit.

You recognized my highest potential.
Your encouragement spoke life into me.
You poured your richness of love into me
and filled me up with the greatest love.

In the physical, you were my best friend.
In the spiritual realm, you're my guardian angel.
The most beautiful gift you've given me is
unconditional love in both human and spirit form.

I love and miss you.
And, I can't wait to hug you tight when I see you!
It's a bashment next time we link up, Mami.

Love is patient. Love is kind.

It does not envy, it does not boast, it is not proud.

It does not dishonor others, it is not self-seeking,

It is not easily angered, it keeps no record of wrongs.

Love does not delight in evil but rejoices with the truth.

It always protects, always trusts, always hopes, always perseveres.

~ 1 Corinthians 13:4-8 NIV

My Intention...

Throughout our lives, we face challenges that present us with choices to either battle against change or push us to the next level in our growth. The tests that come with these challenges can be ugly, dark, and heartbreaking. These growing pains make it difficult to recognize the beauty surrounding and hidden within the imperfections. It's even harder while we're in the darkness, to have a positive mindset and trust we are being guided towards our light.

Self-love looks different for each of us. Each one's journey is personal, imperfectly perfect, and evolves endlessly. My own experiences have taught me to love myself gently with compassion in the light of adversity. I had to change my perspective to change the narrative I was feeding my soul. My intention for *Imperfect Self-Love* is to empower you to love yourself more freely through my revelations. I may not know your story, but I can relate to matters of the heart.

I pray to magnify your light and empower you through *Imperfect Self-Love*.

Welcome to a journey, to the light,
of imperfectly perfect self-love.

May my art resonate with you.

May you see the light in the darkness.

May your tests reveal your resiliency and power.

Walk with me, love with me, and shine your light
down the path of restoring your wholeness.

Table of Contents

High Standards 15
Never Settle for Mediocre Love 16
Superficial 20
Mixed Love Signals 23
Mister Hi & Bye 24
Women, Raise The Bar 26
Dear Black Men 27
Seasons 28
Bloody Legacies 30
Still Single 32
Freedom 34
Narcissist 36
Community Lovers 41
Dropped Jewels 44
Your Highness 45
Guard Your Heart 46
Nothing In Life Is Free 55
The End For Real This Time 58
No, We Can't Be Friends 62
Obsession 64
Dear Younger Self 65

Keep The Same Energy	68
My Type Of Love	76
Royalty	79
Vibe High	80
Inner Child Wounds	82
Chased Love	88
Kings Deserve Love Too	91
Manifesting You	93
Dreams Do Come True	95
I Am	97
Destiny	102
Dear Future	103
Rose Thorns	106
Balance	107
Unbreakable	113
Love Never Dies	116
Prayer For You	118
Healing	119
About the Author	121

IMPERFECT
Self-Love

A Collection of Poems, Quotes & Affirmations

High Standards

Do you love yourself
as much as
I love you?

I created you to be special.
I carefully took my time with you.

Abundance is your birthright.
I placed this principle inside of you.

A blessing is attached to your testimony.
I wish you could see what I've prophesized over you.

                        Signed with unwavering love,

                                           God

Never Settle for Mediocre Love

social media is full of distractions
scrolling
the likes
the comments

tactics to break or
boost up your confidence

though you're satisfied with being single
filled with curiosity
your thoughts sometimes drift to
meeting the one

intense attractions end up as lust
another lesson
a blessing
or a bust

the arguments
the betrayal
breaks the trust

communication fades away
soul ties remain

faced with the decision
to unfollow or block

life goes on
and you learn to be happy
being single again

meanwhile your friends celebrate
engagements
weddings
anniversaries
gender reveal parties

don't allow social media
to become your point of validation

dating prospects who are qualified on paper
yet one box they can't check off
is keeping it real with you

never settle for mediocre love

let go
and let God take control

surrender
hold on to your peace

if God can fulfill his promises to Ruth and Boaz
why wouldn't He set you up for the win
He wants you to shine in all of His glory

never settle for mediocre love

i'm holding on to
parts of you
instead of looking at the bigger picture

your actions disclose
you're emotionally unavailable

the harsh reality is
i must accept
where you are

even
the parts of you
my heart refuses to let go

my mind tells my heart
to leave you alone

bad timing
you're not ready for me
i can't get caught up in your potential

Superficial

back in the day
my preference was
he had to be
tall and cocky
complement my fly

now my standards are higher
i don't compromise my non-negotiables

his level of spirituality
maturity
his character
spirit
loyalty is what truly matters

good looks fade
fall in love with a heart of substance

The mastery of self-love forces you to break out of old cycles and choose powerful interactions that reflect how you love yourself.

intuition is magic
a supernatural
superpower

when you tune in
you can hear its distinctive vibration

honor your heart
intuition leads you to your truth

Mixed Love Signals

the windows to your soul
tell half truths and lies
your words aren't your bond

i slipped up
i focused on your words
more than your actions

blindsided by love
i must face the harsh truth

you're incapable of
loving me
the way
i deserve
to be loved

Mister Hi & Bye

he randomly checks in and pops out

he wants to see if he has access to you at his convenience

don't waste your time with his foolishness

this type of man knows how to provide the bare minimum to continue to be relevant

he manipulates to hold space

that space is meant for somebody geniune

It's not your responsibility to persuade someone to like you or commit to you.

If you have to prove your value instead of showing up as your authentic self, then that person doesn't see the value in you.

Women, Raise The Bar

she doesn't want to be bothered with
the stressors of a relationship
so she settles for the second best option
the side chick

know your value then others will rise to your vibration

Dear Black Men

Take responsibility to seek help for your
childhood traumas and your unhealed chakras.

The foul part is instead of seeking help for your healing,
you project your troubles on to us, women.

The sacrifice of loving you shouldn't break our spirits,
mentally and emotionally.

It's unfair, we end up traumatized
in exchange for your love.

Even after all we've been through,
we see the greatness in you.
We still love you, but now times have changed,
and we must hold you accountable.

Signed with nothing but love,

Black Women

Seasons

thank you for showing me how beautiful love can be
except my love can't be with you

some deep connections are surface level

some relationships aren't meant to last forever

*no matter how much you love someone
sometimes you just can't be together*

truth is —
you're not for everyone

you'll be too extra
too forward
or inadequate

be you anyway

Bloody Legacies

blood joins us together
the disrespect tears us apart

we're family though

we make up excuses for family dysfunction
blood is supposed to bind us together in love

we're family though

when we want to cut ties
family doesn't hold much weight
when it comes to our peace of mind

we're family though

but you leave me with no other alternative
than to cut you off

we're still family though…

relatives are given to us and not chosen
family can be toxic too
it may hurt but still choose you

Still Single

thirty-something

and still single

my ego tricks me

in an attempt

to lose sight of all the blessings i've had

thirty introduced me to a fresh perspective

love without attachment to the outcome

comes around

when you least expect it

still single

but right where

i'm aligned to be

anyone can be in a relationship

we should emphasize how to make one last

my singleness is a choice

often misconstrued

i can't be with anybody

Freedom

i release worry
i release fear
i release self-limiting beliefs

i detach from outcomes because
i have faith in divine providence

finally i'm free

they recognize your light…
become attracted to your light…
and realize it's too bright

if the cost is to dim your light
you diminish your brilliance

Narcissist

in efforts to shut me up and shut me out
you belittle me

the voice you try to quiet is the same voice
you were initially attracted to

during the honeymoon phase
you expressed my sensitivity made me empathic

my vulnerability eventually turned into a flaw
now i'm too sensitive

the attributes you loved
gradually turned into insults

to kill my self-confidence
below the belt comments were used against me

you sought to love bomb me into compliance
i didn't fall in line
and in your own words
i displayed defiance

you tricked me into a fantasy
of what seemed
too good to be true

i'm the one to blame
the more love i gave you
i imagined you would reciprocate

it's a weak power trip
to manipulate my emotions
to coerce me to engage in your wicked game

*you don't know you're dealing with a narcissist
until you deal with a narcissist*

Love isn't manipulative.
Love isn't manipulative.
Love isn't manipulative.
Love isn't manipulative.
Love isn't manipulative.
Love isn't manipulative.
Love isn't manipulative.
Love isn't manipulative.
Love isn't manipulative.
Love isn't manipulative.
Love isn't manipulative.
Love isn't manipulative.
Love isn't manipulative.
Love isn't manipulative.
Love isn't manipulative.
Love isn't manipulative.
Love isn't manipulative.
Love isn't manipulative.

people will want to hurt you

it has nothing to do with you

but more to do with them

broken people break people

hurt people try to fix them

don't give them
a second chance to
tell you
they don't want to
be with you

Community Lovers

you went from treating me special
to treating me like i was ordinary

my love changed
when our laughs
quality time
and the mysterious layers of you
only meant for me
were shared with those
who stroked your ego

i chose you
only you

unaware you were for everybody

the timeframe
it takes to overcome pain
is indefinite

my heart hurts but it's not physical heartache

i cry
i let it out
tears fall

the days turn into months
slowly but not fast enough

on certain days
i find it harder to cope

i pray for the strength
to pick up the pieces

sooner would be better than later
it feels like i'm on pause

i wish i could hit fast forward to see the future

*i want to get back to being in alignment
before i gave you access to my spirit*

Dropped Jewels

time and energy are the new currency

date and eliminate until you meet your soulmate

you won't know what you desire in a lover
until you identify what you don't want
in this dating game

Your Highness

readjust your crown

hold your head high

you must have forgotten the power you possess

they try to conquer you to purposely make it fall

your allure can be seen as a threat

believe in your powerful essence

you're a masterpiece

Guard Your Heart

be selective

guard your heart

for everything you do

flows from it

protect it at all costs

use your discretion

It's impossible to build solid foundations
on lies and deception.

we act like love is disposable

we open up

become vulnerable

we get fed up and push our love to certain limits

we throw the power of human connections away

we run from love and don't fight for love

simply to chase the same feelings in someone new

we repeat this behavior and the love for our new lover

turns conditional too

Love reciprocates.
Love attracts more love.
Love radiates.
Love begets love.

Love is the most energetic force in the universe.
Love raises your vibration.
Give it to yourself first.

when we communicate

let's seek understanding

listen and be slow to speak

poor communication kills the relationship

effective communication helps the relationship thrive

wo(man) and man are complementary

two wholes come together

an imperfectly perfect union

healthy soul ties

two hearts connected to create

their greatest love story

trust the flow of life

love is not linear

relationships change

real love can be built to withstand the test of time

you might fall in and out of love

even get your heartbroken

everything happens for a reason

i pray you fall in love with the person

you're destined to be with

Love cannot flourish in envy, resentment, or bitterness.

Nothing In Life Is Free...

If people do things for you and constantly remind you of what they've done, it's not coming from the kindness of their heart.

she becomes guarded
more apprehensive
when she feels
she's being a fool in love

everyone knows
what's going on
behind the scenes
of her relationship

she protects it
unaware
the joke's on her
because everyone knows
the man she fell in love with
can't be trusted

if you ever put me in a position to choose
my self-worth over my love for you
i'll choose my well-being

love yourself
wholeheartedly
unapologetically
and authentically

don't lose sight of who you are for love

The End For Real This Time...

our normal conversations
consisted of pettiness and toxic arguments

we wanted us to work out
we couldn't seem to get it right

maybe this was God's way of telling us
we weren't meant for each other

whenever you demanded space
i wanted us to talk it out

instead you would storm out the door
to run into the arms of other women

my heart didn't want to admit
what my intuition kept whispering

the red flags became more apparent
when i thought
i wanted to marry you

in the back of my mind
i knew you weren't the one

the life i envisioned with you
slowly faded as our love flames extinguished

the man i fell in love with
no longer existed
i wonder if he ever did

this is the end of us

cherish the memories we've made
to remember me

                                    bye

after the breakups and the makeups
i stayed longer than i should've

my intuition gave me the confirmation
i needed that you weren't my person

i refused to listen and would take you back
i can see why you would lose respect for me

our relationship was officially over
when i couldn't hide behind the lies
you were telling me

when you returned to
correct your wrongs
to make them right
my intuition warned me of the red flags

it was a test i should've passed

a test on repeat
to show spirit
i love me

No, We Can't Be Friends

i wanted to be with you
but you couldn't meet my expectations

i got the less qualified version

no, we can't be friends

you claimed to be in love with me
but we couldn't peacefully end

no, we can't be friends

our story was full of false realities

the man i professed my love to
the man i planned to spend the rest of my life with
revealed his mask
before we made the ultimate commitment

no, we can't be friends

his ugly truth dismantled the version of him
i wanted to believe in
he left me with his mask off

no, we can't be friends

it hit me hard when i realized i fell in love with a fraud

Obsession

when you seek
you find

whatever is in the dark
comes to the light

let go of the attachments
or play with paranoia

spying on their social media
goes from
one last time
to a compulsive
one more time
addiction

an ex is an ex for a reason
maintain your integrity
even when no one is watching you

Dear Younger Self

i'm sorry in advance for the
apologies and closure
you'll never receive

closure is yours to create
progress
Young Queen

in the past i had to see it to believe it

now i believe it when i feel it

trust in the guidance of your intuition

i love love
hopeless romantic

not sure why
the goal was to marry young
i was stuck on a made-up timeline

i was impatient

naïve

my heart was gullible to benevolent acts

i rushed the idea of love
my lower self was infatuated with lust

you can only receive what you desire
when you embody
what you want to attract

spirit sent a message –
stop compromising self-worth
focus on self-love and
rediscover my truth

i'll never settle in my life again

Keep The Same Energy

you introduced me to dope vibrations

in your absence
i crave your bomb energy

i noticed your patterns changed

you pulled back
i withdrew

i miss you
but my pride won't allow me to say it first

damn i wish i could be more like you

i'm conflicted
i don't know how to interact with
this unfamiliar side of you

you're able to disconnect your feelings
you play it off pretty well

keep the same energy you had in the beginning
i'm second guessing the vibe you introduced me to

with the darkness of the world

i need your love to vibrate high

illuminate my life or leave me alone

different love

different efforts

different conditions for
different associations and friendships

different ones require more work than others

different connections

never settle for mediocre love

never settle for mediocre friendships

i'm learning to remove my energy

from people who feel the need to

demean my opinion to validate theirs

God's divine connections are more valuable than worldly riches.

You attract what you believe you deserve.
You attract what you believe you deserve.
You attract what you believe you deserve.
You attract what you believe you deserve.

You attract what you believe you deserve.

Never settle for less than what you deserve.

i don't want what anyone can have

i want what's made distinctively for me

only me

then i will know you were created for me

My Type Of Love

selfless love
patient in love

we caress each other's minds
our souls collide

i believe in you
you believe in me
energy

your other half
an organic type of chemistry

what did i see in you

you're torn between
instant gratification
and long term satisfaction

i ignore my intuition
because you promise me
you'll improve and be a better you

my heart deserves more
i can't be with a player

rule # 717: *i refuse to compete for love*

know thyself to attract your supreme match

filter out those who aren't for you

Royalty

I deserve to be treated with respect.

I deserve to be held in the highest esteem.

My heart deserves to be handled with sacredness.

Vibe High

the energy you put out
returns to you

the energy you attract is a mirror of the energy
you're holding on to

his walk has nothing to do with you

her walk has nothing to do with you

your spiritual walk is personal

Inner Child Wounds

My younger brother and I grew up in a two-parent household. However, in 2011 we were devastated when we found out our parents made the drastic decision to separate. Our normalcy, as we know it, changed. It felt like we woke up one day and our happy home was destroyed.

At the time, therapy was out of the question and wasn't widely accepted. My Jamaican pride wouldn't allow me to seek professional help. I wasn't deep in my spiritual journey, yet. I was also ashamed of what my parents would think of me, if I came across as being too emotional about it.

I wish therapy was welcomed then, instead of being associated with negative connotations. My Jamaican upbringing made me discredit my emotions. I kept my feelings private because I felt helpless. My father always protected me, so feeling helpless was a feeling I wasn't accustomed to. There was nothing I could do to fix or mend their relationship. I wanted my parents back together again.

I swept what was happening under the rug because that's all I knew how to do. It was my defense mechanism. It was my way to channel my emotions. In the West Indian culture, strength represents being mentally strong through extreme adversity.

Based on previous conversations, my father would counteract my biggest frustrations with, "It seh it go" (meaning that's how it goes). I interpreted his words of wisdom as you deal with whatever life throws at you without breaking. These same rules applied in 2011. What was there to talk about besides feeling broken? I couldn't healthily process my emotions because I've never experienced anything of this magnitude. My heart was hurting inside.

My parent's separation played a toll on me. My mornings were a battle. I would wake up angry and uneasy. My escape from reality was to sleep it off. I had no idea I entered a state of depression. I didn't know what to do or who to believe, but asleep was when I felt the most peace.

I didn't understand my dark emotions. For the first time in

my life, I hit rock bottom. I was forced to release and surrender to events outside of my control. I had to figure out what it meant to surrender. I had to step into the new version of me, whether I was prepared for it or not.

From there on, I knew life wouldn't be the same, but I accepted the challenge to persevere anyway. Although my parents didn't stay together in my adult years, I learned to pick myself up and keep chasing my dreams regardless of the plot twist. Their separation taught me to choose a side; I could play the victim or, I could look within and welcome the beginning of my evolution. Needless to say, I chose to walk in my truth to create my peace.

Suffering is inevitable, but I pray for the protection of your peace during the storms.

God sees
God hears
God remembers
God knows

God is omnipresent
God doesn't need your help

When you realize life is a precious gift,
you move to a different beat.

it's tough to remove people out of your life

you question your judgement
become confused with their resistance to
walk out of your life

sometimes people are placed in your life
without your input of
who gets to stay or leave

while you give them passes
and the benefit of the doubt
God will remove them
without your permission
as part of his provision

never settle for mediocre love

Chased Love

you noticed the warnings
his behavior switched up

it felt strange
women know what's up
when their man's behaviors change

his love became distant
she felt alone in her relationship
instead of addressing the elephant in the room
he would turn his phone face down
and come off as suspicious

she finds out what she already knew
he lies about the other woman
she has a gut feeling he's lying

she convinces herself all men cheat
she wants to believe this affair
is his first act of infidelity

she takes him back
he has two girlfriends
wrapped up in a
messy love triangle
without either one of their consent

he has the upper hand in this situationship
he has his ride or die
plus his second girlfriend
who knows who else is on the sideline

heal your heart

love yourself again

a broken heart while dating
leads to repetition of involvement
with the same type
disguised differently

heal and love yourself

Kings Deserve Love Too

He said,

"We're taught to hold back our tears,
silence our feelings
because it's socially acceptable to
'take it like a man'.

Women are known to be emotional
while our insecurities are
suppressed inside.

We want to be encouraged
when our spirit struggles to find the victory.
The outside world views us differently.

We need reassurance all will be well.
You don't understand how difficult it is to be a
Black Man in America.

Queen, our privileges are completely two opposite
extremes."

let's be intentional
to build our union
with principles
to endure
future
disagreements
shortcomings
and hurdles

thrown in the mix
of chaos
to alter
the course of
our hearts
and
mindsets

love can bring out the ugly scars in us

Manifesting You

when we meet
we'll both understand

love over everything

i'll be ready for you
you'll be ready to receive me

you would've already made room for me

our connection will feel
unlike anything
we've ever felt before

we'll continue to date in marriage
i won't let you forget why i chose you
to be my husband

i'm manifesting you

Manifestation is the effect of intention and visualization.

Dreams Do Come True

i love being with you

you give me butterflies

you know when to hold me tight
and i know when you aren't alright

it's been a minute
since i've felt this secure

karma turned my heartaches
into one of life's most beautiful gifts...

the ability to love again

i've prepared the blueprint

it's uniquely designed for you
no one on this earth can do what you do

a blessing is coming
visualize it into your existence

you're headed to a place flowing
with milk and honey

~ **God**

I Am...

I am grateful
I am alive
I am healthy
I am prosperous
I am victorious
I am free
I am confident
I am equipped
I am a conqueror
I am talented
I am beautiful
I am intelligent
I am a child of God
I am spiritual
I am gifted
I am a leader
I am a gift
I am radiant

It's impossible for me to go back to who I use to be.

Wisdom and discernment are essential survival skills.

the law of attraction
will make it seem as if
you attracted the one

amid his observations
the devil will prey on your weaknesses

with God you have the advantage

grounded in spiritual shield protection
before you become emotionally involved

curses can be gift wrapped to appear as blessings
the devil will try to trick pain into pleasures

God won't fool you

confusion and chaos are not of God

In a sexually charged world,
let's bond mentally and spiritually.

I'd rather touch the unseen,
your mind and spirit.

your presence

your warm smile

your embrace

your touch

i'd rather the nonverbals

over what you think i want to hear

Destiny

there's no coincidence
we can read each other's mind
telepathically

your intelligence is mentally stimulating
your energy is a gift

i can't get enough of you

Dear Future

Before we divinely meet, I thank God for you.

XoXo,

Your Eternity

Love starts from within.

Love yourself to the core.

Love the unfavorable parts of you.

Be gentle with yourself, love.

Get the ring, don't chase the ring.

Know the difference.

Rose Thorns

panic attacks
trigger her
unhealed
exacerbated wounds

wound after wound

she's become desensitized
to history repeating itself

her rose petals wither
you might prick your finger
be gentle with her

be the reason why her rose blooms

Balance

everything you are to me

i'll multiply and send it right back out

for you to receive

let's pour love into one another

let's balance each other out

God is trying to guide me
but i want to do it my way

mistake after mistake
i pick myself up and end up
repeating the same mistakes all over again

i go through ups and downs
but it seems there are more downs than ups

i'm angry
i'm bitter
i'm not where i thought i'd be

trying to change the trajectory
how will i mature if i keep pointing the finger
playing the blame game without taking accountability

i have to make the best of what life has to offer
i have what it takes to make it through

i'm not a product of my environment
i'm not what life throws at me

i'm a champion in this ring
no obstacle can defeat me

i have what it takes to make it out any season
dodging these lower vibrations and frequencies

after all this is bigger than me
too many people have my back
and want me to succeed

my emotions don't control me
life has its ups and downs
i have to make sure i always get back on top

life's biggest lessons are those learned
in the darkest of spots

i want to get to know the inner me
the parts unborn and undiscovered

i'm patient with others
it's my time to be patient with me
and show myself grace

i want to face my fears
reveal the secrets i pretend to dismiss
because it doesn't mirror my reflection

i am who i am

Accept yourself for who you are.
Appreciate how far you've come.

Cultivate self-love with grace:

Self-Respect

Self-Discovery

Self-Acceptance

Self-Worth

Self-Awareness

Self-Esteem

Self-Care

Self-Compassion

Unbreakable

I've been lost.
I've been told I wasn't good enough.
I've made plenty of mistakes.
I've slept with demons.
I've been judged.
I've been verbally and physically abused.
I've been combative and defensive.
I've held on to anger for years without therapy.
I've dealt with depression before I could give it a label.
I've been the victimizer.
I've encountered near death experiences.
I've ended friendships I expected would last a lifetime.
I've lost my mom.
I've had panic attacks where I've felt like I was suffocating.
Through these trials, I'm surprised I didn't give up.

*I was in therapy for 4 years before I found the right fit.
I removed myself from people and situations that no longer serve me.
I found self-love in the darkness.
I've restored my confidence.
I no longer suffer from depression.
I've learned to accept my anxiety.
I've learned to let go of validation from others to feel complete.
I've learned to feel through my feelings, both good and bad.
I've learned to hold on to my peace.
I've taken the time to heal, so I don't hurt those who love me.
I survived even when I thought I would remain broken.*

Thank God for resiliency.

More healing.
More love.
More good vibes.

Love Never Dies

From time to time, my mother's voice whispers in my
ear, "you got this, daughter" like she would say any
other time I needed reassurance.
Her constant encouragement left me feeling invincible.

I didn't get the chance to say goodbye forever
to my best friend and mother.
Life's not the same without her.

I was left with an open wound without closure.
Now, the difference is she's by my side in spirit form.

The spiritual signs and synchronicities
direct me on my path to
my healing, my recovery.

I guess that's what they symbolize as strength.
Tears fall from my eyes when my mind plays
flashbacks of her essence.

I reflect on my fondest memories of her
when I see a little girl with her Mommy.

Or, out of nowhere, I think about how she'll be
missing in human form for future celebrations
because if she were here, she would be there.

There's a void in my heart, I'll never get back.
They say it gets easier with time,
but I've found that to be untrue.
Your appreciation for life is placed into perspective.

Life is unpredictable.
God knows who to send to you
for your peace and comfort.

God knows your every need.
He will pull you through.

I promise you!

The beauty is love never dies.

Prayer For You

I pray God covers you
I pray He guides you
I pray your steps are divinely ordered

I pray
He transforms you into your higher self
I pray
He blesses you abundantly

This is my prayer for you
I commend your vitality
for choosing you above all else

God: *I love you, even when you fail to love yourself.*

Healing

Drink water.
Exercise.
Pray.
Meditate.
Repeat affirmations.
Protect your energy.
Detox.
Love on you.
Take good care of yourself.
Relax.
Be playful.
Laugh.
Chill.
Manifest.
Dream.
Attract the life you want.

Nourish to flourish.
The beat goes on in the healing journey.

About the Author

Keisha A. Bloise, M.S. is a scientist within the clinical research arena. She received her undergraduate degree in biology with a minor in psychology from Montclair State University and her graduate degree in Clinical Trials Sciences from Rutgers School of Biomedical and Health Sciences. Keisha was born in the Bronx, New York. She grew up in Yonkers, New York, and has spent most of her life in East Orange, New Jersey.

Her passion for writing came early on, and eventually became a hidden creative outlet of her self-expression and healing. Keisha considers spirituality, family, and laughing uncontrollably to be the most important. Her hobbies include meditation, travel, and sunset and moon watching. One of her mantras in life is, it's in our birthright to love, be love and live a life full of richness. *Imperfect Self-Love* is her first written piece.

For More Information, Visit:

www.TheLoveScientist.com

www.ingramcontent.com/pod-product-compliance
Lightning Source LLC
Chambersburg PA
CBHW070920080526
44589CB00013B/1373